Dachshunds

THE LONG AND THE SHORT OF THEM

Dachshunds

THE LONG AND THE SHORT OF THEM

CAROLINE DONALD

PIMPERNEL
PRESS LTD
www.pimpernelpress.com

Pimpernel Press Limited
www.pimpernelpress.com

Dachshunds
© Pimpernel Press Limited 2020
Text © Caroline Donald 2020
Illustrations © see p96
Design by Becky Clarke Design

A catalogue record for this book is available from
the British Library.

ISBN 978-1-910258-27-9

Typeset in Bliss
Printed and bound in China
by C&C Offset Printing Company Limited

9 8 7 6 5 4 3 2 1

*Crusoe the Celebrity Dachshund, right,
with his half-brother Oakley out on a trek.*

Contents

Introduction

You've opened this book, so we can assume you are interested in dachshunds – aka dachsys, doxies, sausage dogs, wieners, teckels and dackels. And who can blame you? Although some might mock their petite stature – as the twentieth-century American writer H.R. Mencken famously put it, 'a half-a-dog high and a dog-and-a-half long' – those of us who share our lives with these pocket rockets know they are a dog-and-a-half full of character. Once bitten, so to speak, that's it: you are likely to be a lover for life.

Since dachshunds came into my own life in 2012, my house has filled with dachsynalia given by generous friends – as were the dogs (*very* generous friends). Socks, oven gloves and apron, notepads, birthday cards, tea towels, mugs, key rings, a collection of Christmas tree decorations – all are decorated with sausage dogs. I even have an eraser in the shape of one, though am yet to receive a pair of earrings.

'a half-a-dog high and a dog-and-a-half long'

H.R. Mencken

The author with her wirehaired companions Mitzi and Heidi.

This paraphernalia is not just because they are an amusing shape: dachshunds are everywhere, the dog *du jour* and the go-to for advertising campaigns if you want a cute canine – especially the miniature smoothies, which rank among the top ten in the UK Kennel Club's list of favourite breeds. A standard wirehaired dachshund called Maisie (aka Champion Silvae Trademark) won Best in Show at Crufts dog show in 2020 – a first for any dachshund – and promptly celebrated in true dachsy style, by leaving a small present for the judges and 11 million viewers on the green carpet as she did her lap of honour. There are meet-up groups for owners and their canine companions, dachsy cafes, Facebook groups and Instagram stars; walk along any fashionable metropolitan street and you are bound to meet at least one, prancing along on the end of a lead with head and tail held high and a bounce in its step.

So what is about our little sausage friends that makes them so popular? And how can we make the best life for them? That is what this book is all about, based largely on my own experience and talking to other dachshund owners, who have shared their stories here. It doesn't pretend to be the be all and end all of the breed, as there is plenty of serious advice out there on training and the like – but hopefully we will give everyone at least a titbit or two to chew on.

Mitzi and Heidi

I should come clean; I've had a chunk taken out of my own heart, as I share a house with two miniature wirehaired bitches, Mitzi von Schnitzel and Heidi Wirth, whom I am introducing as they will make guest appearances throughout this book. They are half sisters, and, like many sisters, have a love-hate relationship: not best-best friends but very glad that the other one is around. They are also extremely competitive for my affections.

It amuses me how dogs have three layers of personality: at the top, just being a dog, doing the things that all dogs do (and usually involving a bottom sniff); then there are the breed characteristics we humans have spent centuries introducing – in the dachshund's case, to hunt down burrowing animals – and, finally, the individual personalities, which can be so markedly different.

My own pair are like chalk and cheese. Mitzi, a brindle (wild boar in the United States) with a fine set of whiskers, has never been that keen on exercise, and would much rather hang around at heel when out on a walk in the hope that one's pockets have magically filled with biscuits that will somehow drop her way. She is a keen digger, 'helpfully' using her big front paws to start off on a new hole as soon as I even think of gardening, so that my lawn looks something like a badly laid out golf course. She's touchingly loyal and protective of

Mitzi von Schnitzel and Heidi Wirth: half sisters, both keen on having one's whole attention.

her domain, leading the charge if there is a deliveryman to bark at and, to my shame, occasionally to nip at the ankle, especially if he is wearing a hi-vis vest. She is also very partial to her food, though she would argue that her somewhat stout appearance is due to the loose skin around her neck, which is a characteristic of the breed as it helps them wiggle down a rabbit hole.

If Mitzi sees a cat, she will squeal with fright, before slinking off in an attempt to be invisible, and she can't understand why hens don't want to make friends with her. Heidi on the other hand, is the most dreadful hunter, with the 'prey drive' turned up to eleven; she has a fine time chasing both cat and hen and has the slightly longer legs of her Continental heritage (her mother was Russian) to facilitate this. On a walk, she will sometimes follow her nose off into the far distance, deaf to any attempt at recall. She's too fast and determined for anyone to catch but she will always come back – eventually. A very pretty red, with melting brown eyes, a black button nose and teddy-bear paws, she has certain princess-like tendencies, and cannot bear it if someone else is the centre of attention, demanding to be lifted up for a cuddle to ensure that centre becomes her.

An appropriately short history

This breed is no wimp. The vertically challenged shape of a dachshund is not because it has been bred to look amusing and be easy to carry on the bus but, as the German name suggests – literally, 'badger dog' – it was originally bred in Bavaria as a working dog, used by foresters in order to track game, such as deer, badgers, foxes and rabbits. Low to the ground, with a highly refined nose for scent, it could make its way through undergrowth independently, barking loudly as it chased its prey and letting its master know where he had cornered it, keeping the badger or fox at bay until the huntsman had dug it out.

The dogs were introduced into Britain in the eighteenth century, and America in the late nineteenth century, where they came over with German immigrants, and have been popular ever since. So associated with Germany, along with the Alsatian, perhaps unsurprisingly, there was a bit of a blip in their popularity during the First World War in the Allied countries, although tales of them being stoned in the street as 'German dogs' are probably apocryphal. The writer Graham Greene mentions such an incident in his 1971 autobiography *A Sort of Life*, but he reports it second hand, so even this is not reliable.

One advantage of being Germanic in origin, along with most of the royal families of Europe, is that the dachshund became almost ubiquitous in their company: Kaiser Wilhelm II

Genes will out: Mitzi investigates a badger sett.

of Prussia and Germany had a whole pack of them, which accompanied him everywhere, biting at the ankles of those who encountered them. He even built a memorial to his favourite, Erdmann.

Prince Albert brought a smooth-haired sausage, Waldmann, from Saxe-Coburg-Gotha upon his marriage to Queen Victoria in 1840, heralding a long line of royal dachshunds, and, as with Victoria's love of the Scottish Highlands, sparked a craze among the upper and middle classes. They became largely considered as pets in the UK, rather than as working dogs, as they were in their homeland. A Mr W. Schuller of Poland Street, London W1 imported several hundred in the 1870s to stoke the supply and they were popular enough to merit their own class in a Kennel Club show at Crystal Palace in 1873.

The royal love of dachshunds lasted right the way through to Princess Margaret's long-haired Pipkin, whose pairing with Tiny, one of HM The Queen's corgis, heralded the introduction of the 'dorgi' as an addition to the royal pack getting under the feet of visiting dignitaries. Sadly,

'Nothing will turn a man's home into a castle more quickly than a dachshund.'

Queen Victoria

dachshunds seem to be no more a favourite in the British royal family, but Queen Margrethe II of Denmark is keeping up the canine's crowned connections.

Once so strongly associated with Germany, the feisty breed's popularity has spread worldwide; the miniature's compact stature making it popular with those living in equally compact city spaces. The comic potential of a sausage dressed in a costume also appeals to the Instagram audience, although one suspects the dog itself would rather be chasing squirrels in the park than dressed up as Little Bo Peep on the end of a sparkly pink lead.

Instagram star Crusoe the Celebrity Dachshund.

YOU'RE IN GOOD COMPANY: WELL-KNOWN COMPANIONS TO DACHSHUNDS

KAISER WILHELM II

QUEEN VICTORIA

QUEEN MARGRETHE II OF DENMARK

WILLIAM RANDOLPH HEARST

JOAN CRAWFORD

DORIS DAY

PABLO PICASSO

J.F. KENNEDY

OLIVER MESSEL

LOU REED

ANDY WARHOL

SHARON STONE

DAVID HASSELHOFF

DITA VON TEESE

ADEL

DAVID HOCKNEY

CHRISTOPHER LLOYD

JULIAN FELLOWES & EMMA KITCHENER-FELLOWES

Crusoe the Celebrity Dachshund and his half-brother Oakley

TWELVE POPULAR INSTAGRAM ACCOUNTS

CRUSOE THE CELEBRITY DACHSHUND (smooth, Canada, 805.1k) **@crusoe_dachshund**

HATCH AND NICO (long, Japan, 201k) **@hacth427**

MONTY THE MINI DACHSHUND (smooth, London, 178k) **@montyminidaschund**

KINGSLEY, THE KING OF DACHSHUNDS (red long, Australia, 151k) **@kingkingsley__**

CHUTNEY AND BRANSTON (smooth, England, 116k) **@chutney_muttney**

PRINCESS LILO (paralysed smooth, California, 97k) **@prinss_lilo_weenie**

DJANGO THE GENT (red long, New York, 81.9k) **@djangothegent**

DAISY REY (red long, Australia, 86.4k) **@daisy_rey_dachshund**

DOUGIE (smooth, Cheshire, 60.1k) **@dougie.the.mini.dash**

SNOOPY, HONEY, MARLEY AND CANDY (various, Yorkshire, 47.8k) **@snoopthesausage**

MILDRED THE SAUSAGE (smooth, London, 55.9K) **@mildredthesausage**

FRANK AND BETTY (smooth and wire, Yorkshire, 49.3k) **@thehotdogsofhackney**

Crusoe the Celebrity Dachshund

Modesty is not a characteristic one would associate with Crusoe the Celebrity Dachshund, a black and tan miniature, born in Ottawa in 2009. With millions of followers spread over every form of social media you can think of, you can't blame him for having a high opinion of himself. If he is not dressing up as a fireman for a YouTube video (1.02M subscribers) or chasing squirrels on Facebook (3M followers), he is pictured on Instagram (805k followers) flying off for some sunshine in Florida. His first book *Crusoe the Best Celebrity Dachshund: Adventures of the Wiener Dog Extraordinaire* was a *New York Times* bestseller, and he has appeared on Good Morning America and ABC News. He has certainly earned his self-anointed moniker.

Crusoe shares his life with Ryan Beauchesne and his girlfriend Laurence Dionne and the household has now been joined by Daphne, a shaded dapple long-haired miniature cream. His half-brother Oakley, who lives in Toronto, often comes to stay and joins in the capers as Crusoe's wingman. But life for Ryan and Lauren could all have been so different, as Ryan confesses he was not looking for a dachshund in the first place – he wanted a big dog.

Laurence had other ideas and, after a year of persuasion, finally wore him down and Crusoe arrived. 'At first I was embarrassed to walk down the street as a guy with his little wiener dog.' Nowadays, though, the tables have turned. 'What is ironic is that my girlfriend is the one who is embarrassed now, as I am dressing Crusoe up and taking pictures of him in public. She's had to walk away a couple of times, as if she doesn't know us.'

Ryan was working in web design and digital marketing when Crusoe came into their lives and it helps that he obviously has a good sense of humour. Crusoe's adventures started as a blog, shortly followed by a Facebook page. 'I've had a lot of "creative outlet" hobbies in the past, and had no grand aspirations for what it might become.' Crusoe's fame grew steadily over the first year – 'I think the positive reaction kept me very interested and wanting to do more.' And on the ball rolled, until managing and filming Crusoe became his full-time job in 2015.

What is it that has made Crusoe and his pals so internationally popular? 'In terms of their characteristics, they are very much full of quirky and sassy personality,' says Ryan. 'Their physical appearance, being sausage-shaped, makes them funny to watch.' So that's a start, but it does help that Ryan is a dab hand at making daft dachshund-sized costumes.

Here, Crusoe wants to say his bit. 'Dad makes just about all the outfits, especially the more elaborate costume ones, like my police car and fire truck etc. He also modifies teddy bear

clothes to fit me and some of my finer dress clothing is custom-tailored by a woman on Etsy.' It also helps that the sassy sausage doesn't protest about wearing all these outfits. 'Being born in October, my puppyhood spanned the harsh Canadian winter, and so I was being potty trained in sometimes more than -25°C (-13°F) temperatures. Mum and Dad had me wear sweaters and jackets and boots a lot of times, so this early exposure to being dressed makes me very comfortable with it all.' He adds, with customary humility: 'Plus I am known for just being a very chilled and laid-back dachshund.'

It hasn't all been fun and games though, as in 2016 Crusoe underwent surgery for IVDD (intervertebral disc disease), a genetic condition in which the squishy discs between the vertebrae calcify early and bulge out or burst. It was a long road back for the injured sausage, his devoted fans watching every step, as Ryan took him through intensive rehabilitation. But he is returned to form now: slim, trim and fit, as if nothing had ever happened. You can find out more about his rehabilitation and IVDD on celebritydachshund.com/ivdd-info/.

Jumping up and down off beds and furniture does not help dachshunds predisposed to IVDD – actually, it is probably not a great idea for small dogs anyway – so Ryan invented the DoggoRamp (doggoramps.com), which he launched through crowdfunding in 2018. 'There are various ramps on the market that are short and designed for couches, but I was the first to introduce one totally designed for the bed, with railings, adjustable height and an anchor rope to keep it flush to the bed.'

Crusoe and Daphne now charge up and down the ramp and their adventures continue to be watched by millions. Ryan is sanguine that Crusoe's popularity won't last forever, though – other cute dogs will come forward to centre stage as he gets older. 'It is one of those things that is finite in its course, so there is never a day that goes by where I don't appreciate that my job is to spend time with my dog.' Lucky man.

Artists' dachshunds in the limelight

PIERRE BONNARD AND POUCETTES

The French nineteenth-century Impressionist Pierre Bonnard was a lifelong devotee of the dachshund, owning six in succession and, rather unimaginatively, apparently calling them all Poucette. His love for his dogs was well known among his contemporaries, and he was photographed with Poucette (mark VI?) on his knee as an elderly man. Poucettes were often depicted in the domestic scenes he painted, along with his long-time lover Marthe de Méligny, and often sitting up at table. The charming painting to the left, which hangs in the National Museum of Art in Washington DC, arrived as part of the collection of Mr and Mrs Paul Mellon and was labelled *Still Life with Bassett* but a member of staff pointed out that it is more likely a dachshund: the fact that it is waiting for a titbit at table would surely correlate this. To play safe, it is now titled *Still Life with Dog*.

Still Life with Dog, c.1912
Pierre Bonnard
oil on canvas
51.44 x 62.23 cm (20¼ x 24½in.)
National Gallery of Art, Washington,
Collection of Mr. and Mrs. Paul Mellon.

PABLO PICASSO AND LUMP

Lump – which means 'rogue' in German, lived with Picasso at his villa near Cannes for six years in the late 1950s. He didn't actually belong to the great artist but was left under his care by the photographer David Douglas Duncan, whose itinerant lifestyle and large afghan hound were not conducive to dachsy happiness. Lump immediately felt at home with the artist and, looking at David's many photographs of the pair in his book *Picasso and Lump: A Dachshund's Odyssey* (2006), one can see that the two formed a strong mutual bond although, after David had taken Lump away to be treated for a bad back in Stuttgart, he was not returned. Lump died aged seventeen, ten days before Picasso, aged 94 in 1973. The dachshund is also portrayed in Picasso's many interpretations of Goya's *La Meninas*, and looks rather jauntier than the latter's large hound he has replaced in the foreground.

ANDY WARHOL, ARCHIE AND AMOS

Until Andy Warhol got Archie, a smooth-haired black and tan miniature, in 1973, at his boyfriend Jed Johnson's instigation, he had been a cat man. But Archie soon put those days firmly in the past, being carried everywhere with the artist, including business trips and photo shoots, even Studio 54: any questions in an interview that Andy didn't want to answer, he would direct to the dog, whose opinions on Pop Art and the New York social scene of the era are not recorded.

By now firmly infatuated by the breed, Andy and Jed added Amos, a red smoothie, and that heralded the end of the days of Archie in arms. He and Amos would stay at home, away from the flashbulbs and crowds. Amos was portrayed by Warhol, but perhaps his most famous picture of a dachshund is actually Maurice, who belonged to Gabrielle Keiller, a Scottish collector, who commissioned it and later bequeathed it to the Gallery of Modern Art in Edinburgh.

DAVID HOCKNEY, STANLEY AND BOODGIE

Stanley and Boodgie are probably the most famous dachshunds in art, having been the subject of Dog Days, a 1995 exhibition of 45 vibrantly coloured oil paintings devoted entirely to them, as well as a book of the same name, which is still in print. The exhibition was shown first in Los Angeles, where Hockney and the dogs lived, attracting 7,000 visitors in the first four days, and later at Salts Mill in his native West Yorkshire. It was a brave move: the biggest show he had had in seven years, and none of the paintings was for sale. 'They are too intimate, too personal,' Hockney told *The Independent* newspaper at the time.

Hockney set up easels around his house in order to capture the pair going

'I would rather train a striped zebra to balance an Indian club than induce a dachshund to heed my slightest command.'

E.B. White, author of *Charlotte's Web*

about their daily business of sleeping curled up together (they slept in his bed at night), eating or just hanging out. As Hockney wrote: 'This took a certain amount of planning, since dogs are generally not interested in Art. Food and love dominate their lives.' He also wrote of his beloved duo: 'These two dear little creatures are my friends. They are intelligent, loving, comical and often bored. They watch me work; I notice the warm shapes they make together, their sadness and their delights. And, being Hollywood dogs, they somehow seem to know that a picture is being made.'

THE OLYMPIC GAMES AND WALDI

Ok, Waldi was not a real dog but was the cheeky symbol of the 1972 Munich Olympics, the first official mascot for the Summer Games. Designed by Otl Aicher, he was chosen as the dachshund was a popular breed in Bavaria and was modelled on a real long-haired sausage called Cherie von Birkenhof, which the Munich Games Organizing Committee President, Willi Daume, had given to Félix Lévitan, the International Sports Press Association President in 1970. His cheerful pastel stripes were the colours of the Games, which had been chosen to be in marked contrast to the red and black of the 1936 Berlin Games, organized by the Nazis. These Games were to be ones of joy, and the choice of a dachshund was to reflect the attributes of both the breed and an Olympic athlete: resistance, tenacity and agility.

Two million versions of Waldi – soft toy, plastic toy etc – were sold around the world and his shape was also used to mark out the route of the marathon, which ran downtown and through the parks of Munich, the athletes finishing up along the shape of his back before entering the Olympic stadium.

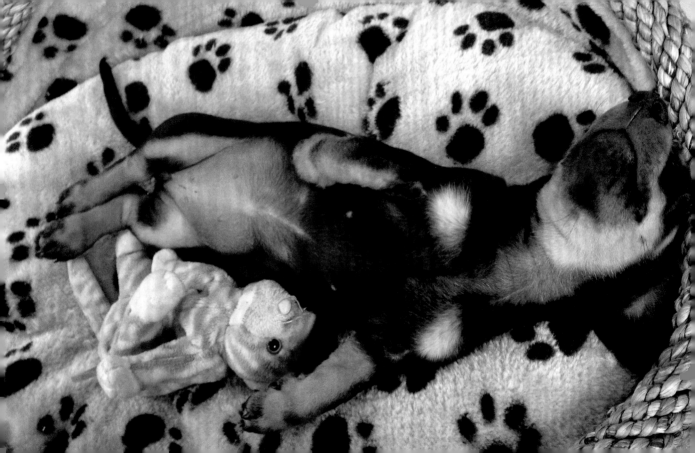

Yoko

Manuela Wirth has always loved dachshunds, and lots of her friends have them. 'I like their independent nature; they are funny and have lots of character. They are not aware they are little and behave like big dogs.'

That she should also mention that Pablo Picasso was a devotee (he shared his life with Lump, see page 28) is apt, as Manuela is one half of the contemporary art world's most influential gallery owners, Hauser & Wirth, which has branches all over the world, including one in Bruton, near where they live in Somerset, south west England. It was her husband Iwan (the other half), who found a black and tan smoothie as a present for her fiftieth birthday. 'We went twice to see the litter and Yoko was the most curious and alert little puppy. I liked her most,' says Swiss-born Manuela.

Yoko, whose name in honour of Yoko Ono was suggested by the artist Pipilotti Rist when she was on a residency at the Somerset gallery, was born in 2013 and came home at eight weeks. 'She slept the first couple of days with our son David, so she would not cry during the night,' says Manuela. Now she sleeps with the family lagotto nero and fox-red labrador, but Manuela admits she is very spoilt, as well as being stubborn. 'The boss in the house is Yoko.'

Manuela is one of Yoko's great loves – 'she is very focused on me, getting loud and excited when I come home. She likes women in general more than men and is not really good with children; she snaps at them.' Her other passion is food. 'She is like a vacuum cleaner and is always hungry – in the kitchen, she is always where we cook, hoping something is falling on the floor.' Sundays brunches are a special treat, as the Wirths' son Bodo bakes a Swiss braided bread called a Zopf and Yoko gets to lick the brush after he has glazed the bread with egg.

Yoko used to eat an egg every day to keep her coat looking glossy but got too heavy and slipped a disc when another dog jumped on her while they were playing. So she had to be put on a strict diet of dry food twice a day, give or take a bone or two with the other dogs. Only Manuela and Shirley, the nanny, dare go near her at feeding time, and she once took on the family great dane Bruno over a piece of meat that had fallen on the floor. For once, Yoko did not have the upper paw: 'Bruno was not amused and got her by the neck. Iwan had to go between them and rescue her. She got away with some stitches and lots of self pity.'

It is not just the kitchen floor that Yoko is patrolling, looking for snacks. 'On our fields we keep sheep and beef animals, fruit trees and our cat places dead mice on our doormat - Yoko finds a way to escape and fill her tummy with all kind of food.' On walks with the other four dogs, Manuela keeps her on a lead, or else she will be off chasing rabbits, squirrels and even deer. 'She has the most amazing sense of smell and is fearless and very fast.' She has even succeeded where foxes have failed. 'We have chicken and there was a time when we found killed chickens in the pen. We were wondering how the fox could get into it, until our gardener saw Yoko running after a chicken, jumping up and killing it.'

The family divides its time between several different bases and Yoko accompanies them, often on a private plane (she has, of course, a pet passport). 'It is not hard to travel with her, but it is difficult to bring her back to the UK, as there are strict rules and you need an airport with a vet,' says Manuela. Yoko takes to these different locations like a dog to water: literally, on one family holiday in Mallorca: 'she jumped into the pool with us and stood on a surfboard,' says Manuela. One cool dog.

Choices, choices

THE GENERAL IDEA

One would be hard pressed to think of another animal that is as diverse in shape and size as the dog, or indeed that the dachshund is descended from domesticated wolves. To each breed its purpose, and although some might think that sausage dogs were just put on this earth to make jokes about, their original role was as a working dog.

Bred from a variety of hounds crossed with spaniels (long-haired) and terriers (wirehaired), they all possess a long snout for following a trail along woodland floors – dachshunds are scent hounds. They also have a deep chest to allow the dog to last for hours underground without having to come up for air, as anyone who has slept with one down the bed can attest. That barrel chest also produces a mighty loud bark, both to alert its human hunting companion and to flush out its quarry. The strong

Be willing to share your bed.

WHAT TO EXPECT

LOUD!

FEISTY

INDEPENDENT

STUBBORN

GREEDY

SCENT HOUND

DIGGER – BEWARE YOUR LAWN

LIKES WARMTH AND CUDDLES – SLEEPING
  UNDER THE DUVET IS DACHSY HEAVEN

ERR, NOT ENTIRELY HOUSE-TRAINABLE

paddle-shaped front paws are perfect for digging and the short legs, loose skin and long body will get them well into the sett or warren without getting stuck. There is always the safety valve of being able to pull them out by their sturdy upright tail, which acts as a flag for owners trying to find them when lost in the undergrowth. Soft floppy ears will stop dirt and seeds getting into the aural canals and protect the eyes.

A plus point for the breed is that they generally don't smell 'doggy'; if they do produce a pong, it may be that they have been rolling in something disgusting and need a bath, or that they have a skin condition that needs attention. A whiff of bad breath when they get to the serious task of cleaning out your nostrils and licking your face can indicate tartar on their teeth, which again should seen to.

Willow

One might expect the dog belonging to one of the world's top creatives to be a beauty and, sure enough, Willow is a pocketful of English cream long-haired loveliness with melting brown eyes. She's the second dachshund to have shared her life with Clare Waight Keller, artistic director of Givenchy, the 'hautest' of haute couture houses, based in Paris. It was Clare who designed the stunningly minimalist white silk wedding dress worn by Meghan Markle at her marriage to Prince Harry in May 2018, now the Duke and Duchess of Sussex.

That was before Willow was born, and before her came Harry (it's a popular name), who lived to the ripe old age of nineteen. 'He was fantastic; what a character. He was an English cream, but he was a "shaded"; they have a little black kohl rim around their eyes, and black tips on their ears and tails," Clare tells me in a brief lull between shows (she had ten per year in pre-Covid 19 times). She bought him when she was living in the States in her twenties, and he went everywhere with her as her career progressed through Calvin Klein, Ralph Lauren, Gucci, Pringle, Chloe to Givenchy – 'he had a bit of a golden passport' she admits.

Nowadays, Clare divides her time between London, Cornwall and Paris, where she works three days a week but, until the Eurostar starts allowing canine companions, Willow remains at home with Clare's husband Philip, an architect, and their three children. At the time of writing, Willow is 'totally in her adolescent phase; being naughty and running off with shoes. She knows exactly what is going to get attention: it is incredibly cute.'

One of Willow's favourite activities is to go for a long run along the sandy beaches of Cornwall. 'She is becoming quite muscular,' says Clare, who lets her go upstairs and jump on and off furniture. 'I have always been a proponent of dachshunds doing whatever they want; I believe, just like humans, the stronger your muscles are, the better it is to hold your back. Up until about fifteen, Harry was here and there and on everything. Then he got a bit slower and we had to help him, but he was doing stairs until about seventeen, and then in the last two years he needed carrying.'

Clare admits that when her husband wasn't around, Harry would be allowed onto the bed. 'He loved nothing better than to be snuggled up very tight against my back or legs on top of the thick duvet and in the morning managed to work his way under the sheets every time. As we started this routine quite young, he then developed a very particular habit of always needing to sleep under a blanket in his own bed, to the extent when he got much older and didn't move around much we could spend ages looking for him, only to discover he was curled up in virtual hibernation under his blanket and not hear us at all.'

Willow has 'so far' not been allowed that bedtime honour: 'She sleeps in her own bed, next to my bedside, never my husband's – definitely territorial there.' In the daytime, when she wants a nap, she has what Clare calls a 'novelty sleeping place – she crawls up my big wicker basket in the hallway, which is filled with coats, and jumps in, hiding deep down in the squishy puffy nylon.'

The much-sought-after English creams have a reputation of being the calmest, most relaxed of the dachshunds, with excellent natures to have around children. Clare would agree with this, and Willow is always by her side as she walks to meetings: 'they are so loyal; very very attentive. I know that whenever I look in Willow's direction, her eyes are locked onto mine and her head is cocked: they are so alert and direct with their attention span. They are just really smart dogs.' One beauty tip Clare let's me into to stop itchy skin is a hemp oil that she adds to Willow's breakfast to make her even more glossy, soft and strokeable.

Despite their sweet natures, both Willow and Harry possess that characteristic many dachsy companions will recognize. 'They have a Napoleon complex: the most massive personality in the tiniest of bodies. They've a bit of a snobby attitude towards other dogs; they definitely don't play with them and, if they do, they get bored within a minute. They know what they are good at, and maybe running around playing is not one of those things. I think there is a regalness about them.'

Vive la difference

'Bold,' 'curious', 'independent': three words that are often applied to our pint-sized pals. But, although there are certain characteristics that are common to all types of dachshunds, such as their heavenly soft ears that constantly need readjusting to default position in a high wind, each has its subtle differences. There are also several colours, ranging from red to black and tan to brindle and cream, with dappled and 'shaded' (an overlay of darker fur) patterned markings. By my reckoning, that gives us over 150 variations recognized by the UK Kennel Club when you add in size. That puts Heinz beans and their 57 varieties firmly back on the shelf, and one is hard pushed to find another breed with so many manifestations. Interestingly, only nine of the colourations appear to be present in all dachshund forms.

Genetics have a large part to play in what sort of puppy is produced in a litter but that is a book in itself for breeders. Suffice to say, all are lovely, though the 'dilute' colours – Isabella (from chocolate) and blue (from black and tan) are not recognized by the Dachshund Breed Council and the Kennel Club in the UK, as the dogs often suffer from CDA (colour dilution alopecia), with thin hair that can make the skin more susceptible to infections and sunburn, which can lead to cancer. They may be rare, but they shouldn't be sought after.

Take your pick: shorthaireds in a variety of colours and markings.

And also on the Kennel Club's no-no list are 'double dapples' (dapples (left) are sometimes known as merles), when dappled dachshunds are bred together: 25% of their prodigy can be prone to multiple health problems, including blindness and deafness. The Kennel Club therefore considers them 'unacceptable' and the pups can't be registered as pedigree dogs. So, if you see a pup for sale with white markings on its head like a collie and blue ('wall') or partially blue eyes, avoid it; it will not have come from a responsible breeder, poor little thing. It could of course be the rare 'piebald' patterned dog but in that case, it wouldn't have blue eyes.

SIZE

Whilst standards (between 7kg (15½lb) and 14.5kg (32lb)) were the original 'badger dogs', the miniatures (under 5kg (11lb)), bred for catching smaller prey, are the most popular. 'Tweenies', which fall somewhere between the two, are also appearing more, but their sizing has not been recognized by the Kennel Clubs of either America or Britain; nor have the 'Kaninchens' (right), teensy tiny little things, weighing no more than 3.5kg (8lb)) that one finds largely in Germany.

DIFFERENT COATS

SMOOTH

The original dachshund, and the most keen on their home team rather than strangers, the smoothies are what immediately comes to mind when one thinks of a 'cartoon' dachshund, with a dense, smooth and shiny coat. The black and tans also have that delightful lighter heart-shaped area covering their hind quarters, like a dartboard for love arrows. While more water repellant than the other coats, it doesn't provide so much warmth, so it would be kind to put on a warm and waterproof jacket in winter: though who needs an excuse? They do look so dashing in one.

LONG-HAIRED

It is thought that this variety came from cross-breeding with a spaniel-type dog in order to ensure a thick coat for warmth in colder climes. It may be cosy, but will need a lot of grooming – up to three times a week. They tend to be long-haired lovers of their owners, sticking close by their side, and calmer and more laid back than the others.

WIREHAIRED

A cross with various terriers – probably dandie dinmonts in the case of the brindles (an old Scottish breed that does bear a strong resemblance to its German 'cousins' and gives them their wonderful beards and bushy eyebrows). The dandie has a soft coat, which sometimes appears in the wirehaired, and this will need regular stripping; it is also not so protective against brambles. Those with 'pinwire' or 'hairy' coats are much more resilient. All wirehaireds have a soft undercoat though, which will need clearing out a few times a year (I use a special comb to remove the dead hair, which the dogs rather enjoy, getting a back scratch in the process), but at least they hardly moult.

Smoothies need to wrap up in winter, though the outfit need not be so jaunty as Crusoe's.

Wirehaireds do seem to be the most feisty and independent – in mine, almost insultingly happy to go off with other people. In some, too, such as my own Heidi, the combination of both terrier and hound genes provides a dachsy with a decidedly 'challenging' attitude to authority when on the scent of a prey and a temporary deafness to a call or whistle overcomes them. Though the scent-hound heritage can come through in any dachshund, it must be said. And away they go, nose to the ground and into the distance.

Missile and Worm

At 6ft 5in (1.95m), one might think that Todd Longstaffe-Gowan would like a dog commensurate with his height, but for the past twenty-three years the internationally renowned landscape architect and his partner Tim Knox, Director of the Royal Collection, have shared their lives with glossy-coated black and tan miniature smooth dachshunds. 'I adore our sausages – whom we refer to collectively as the Booboos. They're bloody-minded and intelligent, and as the adage goes, they're "big dogs in small bodies",' says Todd. 'I grew up with great danes but always wanted a dog one could comfortably hold. There are few things more agreeable than reading a book with a dachshund or two on one's lap.'

Todd and Tim have always had litter sisters. Sponge, their last dachshund, was nineteen when she died, her sister Tiger having preceded her at seventeen, and they didn't hang around to refill the sausage-shaped hole in their lives. They took particular care they got their puppies from a good breeder, who had come highly recommended and whose line had no history of back problems.

Having chosen the pups at about six weeks old, they collected them at twelve weeks and there's been no looking back. Todd poo poos the dire warnings about having litter siblings – they are supposedly inclined to form their own pack, with no room for humans at the top. 'I find that is rubbish,' [it is more of a problem with brothers] says Todd, whose present pair were born in spring 2017. 'They've trained us very well,' he jokes. As with Sponge and Tiger, Todd and Tim each chose a name: Todd selected 'Missile' – 'for she *is* missile-like in the pursuit of her quarry' – and Tim chose 'Worm' for no particular reason, but his decision was informed by the fact that both he and Todd eschew human names for their pets.

Todd reports that the pair get on very well, with few squabbles. 'They do everything together, from curling up in bed to hunting squirrels. It's a very happy arrangement. I'm especially enamoured of their natural symmetry: their heads swivel simultaneously, and their tails wag in tandem, like windscreen wipers.' And they're extremely portable: 'when I carry them, I often stack them like Pringles crisps against my chest' (see right).

The Booboos have been on work trips with Tim to Windsor Castle, though have yet to meet HM The Queen. Having been socialized early, they're good with children and other dogs, as long as they are off the lead, or else they are more inclined to display that loud dachshund bark. Exceptions are made for other dachshunds, which they are always delighted to encounter.

But there is usually someone at home, so the sisters don't have to venture out and are content to sleep by the fire, with each other as company. When Todd gets home, there will be a wiggly and squeaky welcome at his feet. When he picks them up, 'they have that nice pony smell,' he says. "They're utterly life-enhancing, wonderful creatures."

Characteristics

Heidi keeping an eye out for the postman.

TERRITORIAL GUARDIANS

PLUS

You won't ever miss a delivery. Dachshunds are extremely protective of their territory and their deep chests enable a bark that acts as a somewhat discordant doorbell, should anybody approach or even dare to pass. Behind a door or in the dark, this may have the advantage of convincing an intruder that he or she might be dealing with a snarling beast several times larger than reality. Little does the said intruder know that one scoop of the boot under your low-slung guardian's chest and it would go flying.

MINUS

That bark really is loud. This could be a bit of a bore for both you and your neighbours if you are living in a block of flats with people walking by frequently, or if you plan to be out for hours. Put time in with training early on, so that your dachsy has an idea of when you consider it inappropriate to vocalise. Don't shout at it, as this will sound like you are barking too. Be firm though.

There may also be a problem with your pint-sized 'protector' actually taking a bite out of an intruder. We have come to a compromise in my house and there is now a box by the gate so the postman can get in and out of the property before the hounds of hell come running round the corner. However, their bark is generally far worse than their bite, and once they are reassured and out of a confined space, they will roll over for a tummy tickle. That's why dachshunds are called 'watch dogs' rather than 'guard dogs'.

GREED

PLUS

Dachshunds, like labradors, are known for their infinite greed: it's rare that you will meet a picky eater. But surely everyone likes a dog with a good appetite, mini vacuum cleaners who clear their bowls and get rid of scraps in a matter of seconds, don't they? They are also very handy for reaching bits of carrot or crumbs that have fallen under dressers and units that are too difficult to otherwise reach. Friends have had their kitchen floors cleared for the first time in years. One advantage for their owners, too, is that you could leave a lump of raw steak bleeding away on the worktop for hours and it would still be there when you come back into the room: it's another world up there to our short-legged friends.

Being so food-orientated means that a pocketful of treats on a walk will (usually) work wonders at recall and control. Just don't feed them too many, or if they are full, the reward is no longer so enticing. And adjust the size of the dinner offering accordingly later.

MINUS

They won't watch their weight, though, so you have to do it for them: make sure they always have an indented waist like the centre of the figure eight when viewed from above. Overstuffed sausages can get the most terrible back problems, and all that extra mass is carried on very short legs. Viewed from the side, the tummy should be higher than the chest.

As with all dogs, don't feed them chocolate and grapes – especially in raisin form as these are poisonous. As I learnt to my cost (i.e., an expensive out-of-hours visit to the vet when visiting a friend), bags of chocolate coins should be kept well out of the way on a Christmas tree.

The advice, as with all dogs, is not to feed them snacks. In my own case, it is my fault for (occasionally, of course) doing so: one finger in the peel of an orange, or crunch into an apple and in ten seconds I have four brown eyes giving me The Stare at my feet, wherever they have previously been in the house or garden. Mitzi has rather an endearing habit too, of patting me on the back of the (lower) leg when she would like a little snack to keep her going, which one has to say is quite often – it rarely works.

Crusoe decides he has lost half his bodyweight.

PLUS

Although independent in spirit when out on a walk, you will have a very loyal companion, whose great pleasure is to hang out with you, preferably snoozing on your lap or across your chest. What an ego boost, though the latter does make it quite difficult to watch the television.

MINUS

Put time into socializing your dog at a young age to make sure this bond between human and companion doesn't become a problem. Even a few hours alone can be distressing for them without company, so, if you are regularly going to be out at work all day, it is best if you can take him or her to doggie day care, or break up the day with someone coming to take them for a walk: four hours is the maximum time to leave them.

It would be nice to be able to go on holiday for a week or two, too, without feeling racked by guilt that your precious one is miserably shivering in a corner of their billet, so that is another advantage of early socializing. Though it is the other way round with mine: off they go into their lovely homestay kennels to claim their favourite chair without even a backward glance, which is a little insulting, if reassuring.

Crusoe again: always ready for a snuggle.

PLUS

Dachshunds, especially the standards, were bred as working dogs – and in Europe, many are still employed as such (elsewhere they tend to be 'show' dogs, with deeper chests and shorter legs). They may be small but their hunter instinct is still very much there. Watch a dachshund go out for a walk where there are lots of rabbits or interesting smells around. Their nose will be down to the ground, sniffing them out. Even if they aren't on the hunt, there is always a purpose to a dachsy walk: they never scoot around in circles just letting off steam; they are always on a mission.

And, despite their size, they are like little Duracell batteries, happy to be outside for hours and you are likely to give up before they do. It can be quite difficult to get them out though, as some can be rather lazy about getting started, especially when it is raining and there is a warm patch on the sofa to snuggle into. Once they get started though, there is no stopping them.

MINUS

As I have experienced myself, if you have a dog whose hunting instincts are very much to the fore, you need to factor in the extended time you may have to include while they go hunting. It is best to keep such terrors (no names mentioned, Heidi) on a lead if your time is short or there is a road with traffic on it within half a mile of where you are planning to walk and there is a thicket full of rabbits nearby.

Crusoe conquers the world.

What to think about when buying

A dachshund should be low to the ground, with a long back – but not too long, as this will bring problems later – and short legs, not too bandy. The eyes should be bright, the darker brown the better, though some lighter colourings will have amber eyes. They should not be 'wall' eyed (blue, or bicoloured), as this can lead to blindness. Look for a puppy that is engaging without being boisterous (it may be difficult to train), yet not too shy, as the latter may become snappy with strangers in later life.

   Always buy a puppy from a recognized breeder or a household where the parents are known to you. Make sure you can see the mother and watch the puppy interact with her and its siblings. Those bought in a shop may have been bred in a puppy farm under horrible conditions and bring inherited health and behavioural problems. A dog that has come from a happy home and is headed to a happy home is far more likely to be happy and healthy itself.

- They can live until about sixteen. Are you prepared to make that commitment and financial outlay?
- They don't like being left alone for a long time: the generally cited limit is four hours. If you work in the day and dogs are not allowed in on site (perish the thought), is there someone who can give them a walk, or a dog sitter they can go to? This might also entail a financial outlay. A second dachsy as a companion helps combat loneliness but ditto again on the financial outlay.
- These are dogs that were bred to work and need exercise. Are you willing/able to walk them for at least twenty minutes (preferably twice a day?). If not, can you afford a dog walker?
- As the German version of the Kennel Club, the VDH, tactfully puts it: 'It goes without saying that blind obedience is not to be expected'. You can train this dog to some point, but it is never going to be a labrador or a collie, working as a team. It was bred to be independent.
- They can be quite snappy with small children, so introduce the two carefully. Likewise with strangers, so make sure they get plenty of socializing when young.
- How tolerant are your neighbours? That bark is quite loud, though with a well-trained dog it is usually only used territorially when someone is walking by or comes to the door, rather than yipping away all day just for the sake of it.
- Make sure the dog comes from a line that doesn't have epilepsy in it, or congenital back problems. It may mean that it is initially more expensive, but think of the vet bills you will be saving later.
- And remember those vet bills: dachshunds live a long time, but age can bring its health problems. On the other hand, they don't eat as much as bigger dogs (well, they would if you let them), so you are saving there.

DNA TESTING

There are some conditions that are inherited, largely in miniatures; a good breeder will provide proof that their puppies have been tested for Cord1 mutation PRA, which causes degeneration of the retina, resulting in visual impairment or blindness. Mini wires should also be tested for Lafora disease, which is a form of epilepsy.

Heidi's great amusement is to test the 'indestructability' of her toys.

Greta

The odds are pretty high that, when you have moved to the country with four children – in this case Wiltshire, in the west of England – they are going to start nagging for a dog. Thus it was for landscape designer Catherine FitzGerald and her husband Dominic West, the actor best known for his lead roles in the American dramas *The Wire* and *The Affair*.

Dominic kept looking online at 'puppy porn', as he called it, threatening to get a Hungarian vizsla, which would be far from easy to squeeze in with the family on a ferry-bound car to Ireland in order to spend time at Glin Castle in County Limerick, Catherine's ancestral home.

Perhaps Dominic did this to prepare his wife for a worst-case-scenario because, just before Christmas 2019, he arrived home (unannounced), not with a 25kg (55lb) vizsla, but 'carrying the teensiest, tiny mini dachshund puppy, aged about eight weeks,' remembers Catherine. The family called her Greta, in honour of Greta, the girlfriend of Pretzel, the extra-long sausage dog hero of Margret and H.L. Rey's American children's classic, written in 1944.

Although Greta, a black and tan smoothie, largely belongs to the couple's youngest, Christabel, all the children compete for snuggling up on the sofa with her – again, there wouldn't be much room with a vizsla. 'She loves them all and they really love her,' says Catherine, 'she is so happy.' Being outside in the sunshine is her favourite: 'she came to us in the dead of winter and really hated going out but, when it is warm, she and the children play all day.'

Although portable and a great dog for a gardener to have by her side, in that she won't squash all the plants, Greta is displaying a couple of decidedly dachsy characteristics that Catherine is not so keen on: barking at those outwith the family group who dare to enter her territory and – to put it daintily – taking a while to establish a toileting routine that doesn't involve a visit to a precious carpet. At which, Dominic starts muttering again about the joys of vizslas, however hard they may be to squeeze into a car bound for Glin.

Life with a dachshund

BRINGING YOUR PUPPY HOME

Is there a sound more heart-wrenching than the whimpers of a puppy on its first night in a new home? But don't give in! It has to learn that it is safe in its new nest and that you will return in the morning. A crate covered in a rug is good: you can shut it for the night and it is a 'burrow' for the dog. The crate will also act as a refuge from the world when the puppy needs a rest during the day. Donate an old, unwashed jumper to the cause too, so it has a familiar smell to snuggle into.

DACHSY-PROOFING YOUR HOUSE

The repeated word from the manuals is not to let your dachshund on the stairs – certainly for puppies – as this places a great strain on its back. Easier said than done with those canine companions who want to come up to tell you it is breakfast time. A child's stair gate may be the answer, if not very sightly, or, as I have, a panel of lightweight chipboard I take with me when we are going to houses with steep staircases. When put across a bottom step, the dogs can't see over it, so accept they can't get past – in new territory, they soon learn that some places are out of bounds. It is also good for putting across a

Ready to face the world.

doorway when you want to bring in fresh air but not let out your dachshund.

There is a school of thought though, if the stairs aren't too steep, that it is actually good for their backs to get the exercise going up and down them. But wait until after the puppy stage at least.

And whoever succeeded in keeping a dachshund from making a nice warm nest on a sofa? A stool or even steps will help them up, and hopefully down, rather than jumping off when the postman arrives and risking slipping a disk. You can even get little ramps to help them on to a bed. All are widely available online.

Remember these little sausages can squeeze through very small holes, so make sure your garden has been 'puppy proofed' with chicken wire if there are no solid boundaries. It doesn't have to be very high, for obvious reasons.

TOILET TRAINING

Let's be honest: dachshunds are not known for their good house training. If there is a sofa to nip behind, especially if it is raining outside, off they will go. I have to check the far side of a bed in the spare room before guests come for the weekend as that is a favourite spot for leaving a little welcome present for them.

With luck, your breeder will have taught them to use paper for such matters, which you can later put down for overnight stints, if you are in a flat without a garden, or if they are in an unfamiliar place. Otherwise, start as you mean to go on, by frequently taking your puppy outside to a particular spot (every two hours when they are young), or on to the paper and praising them when they perform. If you say a word – 'outies', 'pee pee' or whatever – whilst they are doing it, then hopefully in time, they will perform to command. Then, if outside, let them have some time to sniff around and enjoy being there.

Accidents will happen though, so always keep a bottle of soda water or specialist cleaner handy in order to neutralize the smell. Otherwise they will keep going back to their favourite pee spot.

Dogs on tables is strictly not allowed – though Mitzi argues this is in the greenhouse.

If your dog has been trained to pee on paper, be prepared for it to think that rugs and bathmats are fair game. And to accept that sometimes the paws will go on the paper, but the bum might not quite have reached it. Well, at least they tried.

SHOW THEM WHO'S BOSS

As with children, good manners need to be taught. This doesn't mean you need to shout at the little darling (human or canine), or use corporal punishment, but the dachshund is known for its feisty independent spirit and getting it to obey simple commands – sit, stay, no, come, etc – not only makes your life easier but is ultimately for the dog's own safety. Changing the tone of your voice helps too of course – a low stern NO can often jolt them into obedience. You just have to lose your inhibitions! You need to show your puppy that you are the top dog in the pack; if not, you will just make trouble for yourself, as he or she will assume it is their rightful place to assume that role. They are quick to learn – you have to make it worth their while though, or else they may ignore their lessons. Praise is probably not going to be quite enough: a tasty treat will be needed.

Possessiveness can be a problem, with food, toys and their 'human'. For the former, feed the puppy in instalments at meal time, taking the bowl away after it has finished each helping and replenishing it, so it learns to trust that there is more coming rather than being deprived. Don't give it the food until it is sitting (often quite difficult to tell, as they are so low to the ground), and then put the bowl down with a cheery 'ok!' as an instruction they can get tucked in. An 'all done!' at the end of the meal signals that's it for the moment. Any growling towards others over toys can be dealt with the same way: remove the toy until that lip has uncurled.

When feeding in a group, I also come to the youngest, fastest eater last, having made them all sit and wait for their food until I let them at it (again, just lift the bowl away until they do what they are told). By the time it gets to the turbo-feeder, the others are nearly finished. She soon catches up and this gives the others time before she is snaffling around their bowls, just in case they might have left anything. Fat chance.

Of course, one should not encourage begging. But I would be a hypocrite to say I have not occasionally found that a little piece of apple or crust might possibly have slipped under the table, with the justification to myself that man has been doing just this for millennia. Just make sure those little titbits don't have sugar in them, as those dachsy teeth are precious.

As to being snappy with those who are not the Favourite Human, again, this needs to be nipped in the bud. Socialize your puppy early, with other dogs, children, adults, cats (if you have them in the house), whatever. Be careful with young children, as they might drop that precious little package and don't let them play too roughly with the new arrival. Give the pup lots of time to rest quietly in their crate between bouts of fun and games.

Reading time is Heidi time.

BARKING

It's loud! Stop the barking, especially when you leave them. You are the pack leader, not them, and this they need to learn. If your puppy barks too much when someone comes to the door (and it is actually quite useful to have a canine doorbell), put them in a quiet room until they shut up. The visitor can then give them a treat or make a fuss about them when they are allowed out. Nip excessive barking in the bud when the dog is young, or it will become habitual.

Likewise, if you don't want your dog to rule your life later on by its behaviour – nervous or aggressive – spend time when it is a puppy taking it out to different situations (after all its injections of course): the railway station, a park, to other houses etc. You can even get a recording of noises such as a washing machine, an aeroplane or helicopter going overhead, fireworks etc, which you can play quietly at first but then turn the volume up little by little, so they get used to the noises. It worked on my two – although, rather than being nervous about thunderstorms, they protest loudly at Thor's intrusion on their territory.

WALKIES

Even if you live in a flat in the centre of a city, remember that dachshunds were bred as working dogs, not lap dogs, and should be walked every day, even if they protest and say the rain will spoil their hairdo. They need to keep those muscles strong to protect their backs, and if they get bored and restless at home, it can lead to destructive or needy behaviour. Let them get outside for at least twenty minutes, twice a day in order to sniff new smells and experience new spaces. If you can trust him or her off the lead, you can practise recall and throw balls for them to fetch, with a snack as a reward. Puppies of course should be gradually introduced to walks; their bones are still soft.

GOING DEAF

Heidi, like many of her breed, is a terrible hunter, with a rabbit, a mole and a young cockerel already on her trophy wall. Usually she is fine on a walk and will come back, especially if there is a snack in store: I carry a tube of delicious liver paste that she has to come close to me to taste, and then I can grab her by the collar and get that lead on. A ball will also keep her amused. I was going to say nothing could be more heaven, but a thicket of bunnies beats even liver paste and a bouncy tennis ball, and into it she will dive for hours (well, it seems that length of time when I am waiting). Thus the 'stubbornness' and 'tenacity' of the dachshund manifests itself.

I've learnt not to let her off an extending lead in dangerous areas when I have an appointment within the next two hours, or it is sod's law that she will vanish. Unlike larger dogs, this is not a breed for panting or thundering around on heavy paws when running around, and so can be difficult to locate, as they are so quiet, apart from the occasional excited yip when giving chase.

If your darling is inclined to scarper off on a hunt, fit it with a collar with a cat bell on it. Not only will any nearby rabbits or squirrels be alerted, at least you can hear their location. It also helps build up trust, too, as you don't keep on having to turn around to check where they are. The sound of a tinkling bell getting ever nearer as you stride across a field is a heartening one.

The Dixter dachshunds

Following in the tradition of the house, Aaron Bertelsen's bitch Conifer, left, likes to guard the drive at Great Dixter, the home of the late Christopher Lloyd, who died aged 84 in 2006. Not only was Christo – as he was known – one of the UK's most beloved writers and gardeners, he was also the stalwart companion of a succession of black and tan standard dachshunds, which were as much a part of Great Dixter as Edwin Lutyens's restorations, the sunken garden, the meadows and the exuberant borders.

Christo's dachshunds, which accompanied him everywhere in the garden, were known for being snappy with those they didn't care for. 'I don't want to completely blame Christo', Aaron says, 'but there was a big part of him that liked that about them' – the great man himself could be somewhat dismissive of those whom he felt were wasting his time.

When Christo died, Aaron, who runs Dixter's vegetable garden and has published *The Great Dixter Cookbook*, took on his last pair of dachsys – Canna and Yucca – 'Yucca was kind of mine anyway' – and his attachment to the breed has continued from there. He has continued the tradition of a hugely popular annual Dachshund Day in one of the fields, with agility trials, races and, of course, barbecued sausages. Nothing, however, is taken too seriously: 'I just wanted a fun day when everyone meets up.'

These days, taking a bite out of one of the 50,000 visitors who come to Great Dixter every year (greatdixter.co.uk for details) is not really the form, and Aaron assures me that Conifer would never dream of doing such a thing. He believes it is all in the early training, which wasn't something Christo went in for. 'Dachshunds are very, very stubborn; they think they are far superior to everyone and you have to remind them every day who is in charge.'

So Conifer – who is a solid girl, 'built like a German tank' – is not allowed to sleep in his bed, which she had managed to do for the first few months since her arrival, arranging herself rather uncomfortably over Aaron's neck. But the banishment is not that far: she has her own cosy bed on the floor by the bed, on sheepskin rugs with a quilt that matches Aaron's own. It might soon be a pillow case covered in dachshunds. 'I probably have one of the biggest private collections of dachshund memorabilia known to mankind,' he confesses.

Although all these Dixter dogs are named after plants but it wasn't always so, says Aaron. 'The early ones were called things like Sweetie Pie and Lovey Dovey but Christopher realized that you couldn't tell a dog off with a sweet name.' So, there was some discipline after all.

Health and well-being

Dachshunds are a pretty healthy, low-maintenance pack, often living to a great age. Despite their size, they are an energetic lot and love exercise, often lasting as long on a walk as their human companions. Though, it has to be said, it may take some persuasion to get them out in the rain. They will need a decent daily walk and if there is somewhere safe to let them off the leash, running around after balls etc will also help burn off some energy.

As with all dogs, picking a pup is not just a case of spotting a cute picture on the internet and buying it from there. It is essential to buy from a reputable breeder, or from someone known to you who knows the bloodlines of their dogs. There are some inherited problems that must be avoided if you want to have a happy, long-lived companion. Also make sure it has had all the correct vaccinations before you collect your new arrival, and keep it treated henceforth against the likes of ticks and roundworm. Those little pills one buys regularly from the vet (a good vet will send you out a reminder) are expensive, but less so than the treatment you would need if your dog was affected.

And, speaking of treatments, you may feel it is worth insuring your pup: payments start off quite low, and, of course, as soon as you claim, it will go up. Personally, I now put aside a bit of money every month into a savings account after the insurance premiums

Bright eyes are a sign of good health.

skyrocketed after Heidi broke her leg when she was young. I'd much prefer to build up a fund of my own.

BACKS

It is obvious from their shape that dachshunds might have back problems and, while a fit and muscular dog on a good diet is less prone to these, the breed does demand extra care. Steep staircases should be blocked off, especially for puppies, and older dogs.

You should also be very careful how you pick them up, doing it with both hands and supporting the dog under the chest. Watch out for over-enthusiastic young children trying to pick them up, as they are easy to drop! It is best, of course, to discourage the dachshund from jumping on and off high furniture, but can sometimes be easier said than done – early training not to is the best way. Otherwise, a ramp or a stool will at least provide some help. Again, some jumping may actually be beneficial to muscle tone; just not from a great height.

Watch those long backs; keeping your dog strong and healthy will help.

IVDD

IVDD (intervertebral disc disease) affects about a quarter of dachshunds, through inheritance, elongated shape, neutering under the age of one, or obesity. It is when the squidgy discs between the vertebrae calcify at a young age and either burst or pop out – it can result in paralysis of the back legs, or, worse, can be life threatening if the disc is cerebral. As it is often inherited, check with the breeder if it is in the line. There is hope, though, if your dog is affected; it just takes a lot of painstaking rehabilitation (see Crusoe the Celebrity Dachshund's story on page 24 for links to more information).

If your dog food doesn't already have it, many people add a little cod liver oil to their supper; in a recent survey, those who were fed this, had half the rate of IVDD.

WEIGHT

Few are the dachsys who are picky eaters and it is easy for them to put on weight, which not only makes life uncomfortable for them but lays them prey to the same conditions as humans: diabetes, heart problems etc, as well as a terrible strain on those little legs and spine (I once saw a dog waddling along, its tum about 1cm (½in) from the ground; it all looked a terrible, undignified effort). Keep a firm eye on their diet and make sure they have a nipped-in waist like a figure of eight when viewed from above. Their tum should also be nice and firm, higher than the rib cage when you look at the dog from the side. You should be able to feel the ribs, though if they are showing, along with the spine, then the dog is actually too thin.

It is stating the obvious, but if you feed them at table (no, surely not?), or hand out treats as rewards for good behaviour, adjust the amount you give them for supper that night. If you use kibble, you can even measure out the day's food in the morning, and take some in your pocket for that day's walk and rewards.

TEETH

Dachshunds are prone to bad teeth, so if you can start them off as a puppy with a good cleaning regime, you will be doing much to prevent later problems with the build up of tartar and dental decay, and have a dog with sweeter breath. That said, it is easier said than done but getting some lovely meaty-tasting doggie toothpaste (never use human) and rubbing it around the mouth without a brush at first, will help the dog get used to your finger being inside the mouth. Then, once he or she is used to that, you can introduce a toothbrush, or one of those little finger gloves with bumps on them you can get from the vet.

Feeding them dry kibble instead of wet food is another way to prevent the build up of tartar, as are dental doggie chews; but just remember that those chews contain calories, so adjust the day's allowance accordingly. You can also take the dog to the vet once or twice a year to get the tartar removed; an expensive jaunt, but prevention is better than a painful tooth otherwise.

'**Keeping those teeth clean and the breath fresh is a challenge.**'

River the Mini Dachshund

River the Mini Dachshund lives with Mia Riekert on Australia's Gold Coast. A beautiful miniature long-haired red, she has attracted a worldwide following on Instagram and Facebook. Born in 2015, she was Mia's first long-haired dachshund and she didn't even know about the long-haired ones 'until I got familiar with Peter Alexander [Peter is 'the Pyjama King' of Australia] and his adopted dog Penelope, who features through his brand'. So she started contacting breeders – she was on more than ten waiting lists. 'Six months later, River was born.'

It was love at first sight. 'I've established a connection with her that I've never had with another dog. She is quite a little character – full of personality and adventure and one extremely cheeky girl! She is very independent.'

When Mia goes to work, she drops off River at her mother's house, where Sebastian, another long-haired red, lives. A couple of years younger than River, 'he is a major mama's boy; very soft-natured, cuddle and ball obsessed,' says Mia. River is the top dog in the pair: They are, however, best friends. 'I took River with me with the day we picked Sebastian up, so they met on neutral ground. She instantly embraced him and became a motherly figure by his side.'

Mia's mother's house is air-conditioned and they stay inside all day. 'It gets way too hot and humid in Australia to leave them outside. I stop off most days on my lunch break to give them some outside play time.' As River's Instagram feed shows, they both love water. 'With a gated pool at Mia's mum's house in which to cool off, the most important thing was to train them as puppies to swim straight to the steps, so they knew how to get out in case of an emergency or accident. Sebastian loves the pool so much that he jumps in after his ball, head underwater and all – and he will keep going all day, if allowed the opportunity.'

'We prefer going to a beach most weekends. We always have a shelter set up, so that the pups can lay in the shade when they're not in the water or playing in the sun. There's usually a breeze too, which helps combat the heat and they adore running into the ocean to cool down.'

Sharing her dachsys is a hobby for Mia. 'I mainly take photos for social media over the weekends when we are on adventures. Both love the camera and get excited when I take it out of the bag, as they know treats are coming their way.'

Although River and Sebastian are both reds, their coats are very different. 'It is amazing how many different shades of red there are,' says Mia. 'Sebastian was a lot lighter when he was a puppy. River's coat is quite fine, whereas his is a lot thicker and longer. He visits a professional groomer in the summer months for a little trim, nothing too drastic.'

Useful contacts

THE KENNEL CLUB UK
The world's oldest kennel club, which also organizes Crufts, one of the world's most important dog shows. It is also where you will find breed standards, register your pedigree, find a pedigree puppy, information about health and generally learn about characteristics of the different breeds, as well as information about events. **thekennelclub.org.uk**

AMERICAN KENNEL CLUB
See above for information on the various breeds and registering, but Stateside. Also promotes the annual Westminster Kennel Club Dog Show in New York, and other shows nationwide. **akc.org**

THE VDH (GERMAN KENNEL CLUB)
For those wanting to go back to the dachshund's roots, the VDH supervizes more than 250 breeds and sets standards for 32 of these, including the Teckel (dachshund). **vdh.de**

DACHSHUND BREED COUNCIL UK
Lots of useful information for those thinking of buying a puppy and how to look after it, as well as health and characteristics. Also has a list of breed clubs around the country for those wanting to pursue this further. **dachshundbreedcouncil.org.uk**

DACHSHUND CLUB OF AMERICA
A member of the American Kennel Club, doing what it says on the can, the DCA promotes the health and well-being of the dachsy, upholding breed standards and holding shows around the country. **dachshundclubofamerica.org**

NATIONAL DACHSHUND COUNCIL AUSTRALIA

An affiliate of the Australian National Kennel Control, the NDC has lots of info about dachshunds, member societies and shows. **nationaldachshund.org.au**

DEUTSCHER TECKEL KLUB

Founded in 1888, the German Dachshund Club has 20,000 members and gives plenty of information, including on the kaninchen or rabbit size. For those whose German is not up to scratch, Google's auto translation provides some amusement – apparently the first dachsys were 'shorthaired lizards'. **dtk1888.de**

SUNSONG DACHSHUNDS

Ian and Sue Sneath are UK breeders of champion wirehaired and mini smoothies, but have produced a very useful website about the breed in general, including a list of UK Facebook groups. **sunsong.co.uk**

YOU DID WHAT WITH YOUR WIENER?

American website dedicated to showing how sporty the little sausage can be: hiking, camping, he will be there. There's also lots of useful information about health and care. **youdidwhatwithyourwiener.com**

CRUSOE'S CELEBRITY IVDD INFORMATION

For those who missed the line on Crusoe the Celebrity Dachshund's chapter, having suffered from the debilitating intervertebral disc disease himself, Crusoe and his companion human Ryan have put together a fact sheet about the disease and how to treat it. **Celebritydachshund.com/ivdd-info**

Only a dachsy companion would understand

DACHSHUND CAFE
Weekly pop-up dachsy events touring restaurants around the UK. There are also events for pugs, Pomeranians and French bulldogs – it's easy to tell which are the fashionable breeds.
pugcafe.co.uk

DACHSHUND COUTURE
Handmade outfits in nine sizes made especially for dachshunds, including a very smart Bavarian Loden coat with a silk lining for $300.
dachshund-couture.com

HYDE PARK SAUSAGE WALKS
Monthly walks around Hyde Park in central London, organized on Instagram.
#hydeparksausagewalk

KEY WEST ANNUAL DACHSHUND PARADE
Down at the southernmost tip of Florida, it would seem that what is considered a dachshund is somewhat loosely translated, but it's New Year's Day and everyone obviously feels pretty laid back about such details.
https://www.facebook.com/Key-West-Dachshund-Walk-161327957238019/

KLEINE RESIDENZ (THE LITTLE RESIDENCE)
Situated in one of the central squares of Passau, Bavaria, this is a museum dedicated to all things dachsy, which opened in 2018. There are 4,500 objects collected by the owners, with plenty more waiting behind the scenes.
dackelmuseum.de

MARSZ JAMNIKÓW

Annual September costumed march of thousands of dachshunds (they sure are popular in Poland), many dressed in silly costumes. Organized by Radio Krakow.

radiokrakow.pl

POSH TECKEL

Situated in Berlin, this hostelry calls itself a Manchester Bar, playing the music of Oasis and the like. It is called after the owner's dachshund, which is very much in evidence and much celebrated.

poshteckel.de

SAUSAGE DOG HOTEL

Located in Berkshire (or should one say Barkshire), England. Lots of country walks with dachsy residents Stanley and Ollie.

sausagedoghotel.com

SAUSAGE DOG SANCTUARY

Join Oswald and Betty, the resident dachshunds, for day care or overnight stays in Derbyshire, England. It even makes its own food.

sausagedogsanctuary.com

TECKEL HOTEL

Take your sausage friend to breathe in the fresh air of the Austrian Tyrol.

teckelhotel.com

Acknowledgements

A thousand thanks to those dachshunds and their companions who appear in the book. While an honourable mention should be made of my dear departed father and Flora, his mini wire, who was his faithful companion to the end, this book is dedicated to my book club – Nellie Ashford-Russell, Tessa Coleman, Louise Dowding, Tamsin Graham, Guy Kennaway, Fiona Loveridge, Caroline Mann, Catherine Milner, Bundle Piper, John Robbins and Maymie White, with London branch member Gabrielle Tregear – who decided that it was time I had something to look after and gave me Mitzi for A Big Birthday. With huge thanks to them for that, and for putting up with the little presents left in gratitude by The Book Club Dog in return. And also to Iwan and Manuela Wirth for Heidi-nee-Honey, the pocket rocket, who joined us later; she too has shown her appreciation in many households.

Much gratitude is due to Suki and David Posnett, Melanie Cable-Alexander and Martin Redwood,, Jane and Anthony Hodges, Zoe Stewart and Tiffany Bramley for their stalwart care of the duo; not easy at times but they are all much loved by them.

And lastly, to Anna Sanderson and the team at Pimpernel, dog lovers all, we thank you for your patience! The author may be barking but she is appreciative.

PICTURE CREDITS

Front cover Shutterstock/Shedara Weinsberg; Back cover Shutterstock/Stiglincz Gabor; Endpapers Shutterstock/Denis Sazhin-Iconka; Title page Shutterstock/Valeria Head; Title verso Ryan Beauchesne; 6 Gill Dickinson; 8 Pacets; 10–12 Pacets; 15 Ryan Beauchesne; 17 Pacets; 18, 20, 23, 25 Ryan Beauchesne; 26 Collection of Mr and Mrs Paul Mellon, National Gallery of Art, Washington; 30 © / Comité International Olympique (CIO)/PETER, Grégoire; 32, 35–36 Manuela Wirth; 38 Pacets; 40, 43–44 Amelia and Charlotte Keller; 46 Shutterstock/Liliya Kulianionak; 48 Shutterstock/a katz; 49 Shutterstock/ Liudmila Bohush; 51 Ryan Beauchesne; 52 and 55 Todd Longstaffe-Gowan; 56 Pacets; 59-61 Ryan Beauchesne; 62 Shutterstock/Radomir Rezny; 65 Pacets; 66 and 69 (left and middle) Dora West; 69 right Catherine Fitzgerald; 70 Shutterstock/Gorlov Alexander; 73 Pacets; 75 Pacets; 76 Shutterstock/ NORRIE3699; 78 and 81 Aaron Bertleson; 82 Pacets; 85 Shutterstock/Radomir Rezny; 87 Shutterstock/Csanad Kiss; 88 and 91 Mia Riekert.